Broken

Broken

H. Waldon

Alex Zandrea Books

BROKEN

Poems by

H. Waldon

To those who feel broken.

And to those who inspired me to finish writing
this collection.
It was a struggle.

CONTENTS

CONTENTS

CONTENTS

CONTENTS

This collection is in no particular order or parts like "Damaged" was. It is themed around feeling broken and the thoughts that crossed my mind during that phase of my life. Each day I feel a little less damaged and broken.

DAMAGED

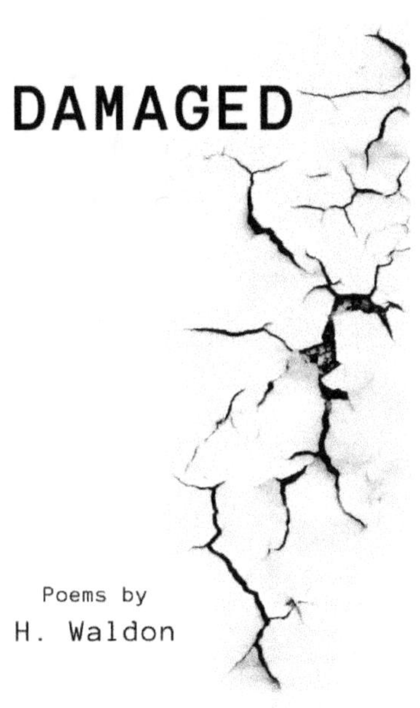

Poems by

H. Waldon

I'm Sorry

In the tempest of emotions, a turbulent sea,
I sailed through madness, lost in a plea.
"I'm sorry," I whisper, the words in the air,
As you treated me callously, with a cold, distant stare.

In the dance of chaos, I spun out of control,
Caught in the whirlwind, my heart took its toll.
"I was crazy," I admit, as the storm raged on,
Yet your cruelty persisted, like a lingering dawn.

Apologies hung in the air, heavy and thick,
A desperate symphony, a sorrowful pick.
For in the depths of my madness, I sought a reprieve,
But you, unmoved, continued to deceive.

I spiraled through madness, a tempest untamed,
Yet your indifference, like a dagger, remained.
"I'm sorry for the chaos, the tumult within,
But your treatment, my love, was an unforgiving sin.

In the mirror of remorse, reflection's embrace,
I see the shadows, the torment I chase.
Apologies echo, a haunting refrain,
As I navigate the wreckage of love's bitter terrain.

So forgive my craziness, born of despair,

A response to the wounds that you failed to repair.
"I'm sorry for the chaos, for losing my way,
But you, in your cruelty, led love astray."

If I Cry

If I cry in front of you, it's the unraveling
Of the fortress I've built, the silent battling.
In teardrops, echoes the weight of my soul,
A vulnerability, a tale left untold.

If I cry in front of you, feel the tremor,
A seismic release of emotions I remember.
The dam of composure begins to decay,
A flood of emotion, washing fears away.

If I cry in front of you, witness the ache,
The storm within, the quivering lake.
Each tear a chapter, a story unspoken,
A heart laid bare, the armor broken.

If I cry in front of you, grasp the depth,
An ocean of feelings, a silent breath.
In the reservoir of tears, emotions dive,
An admission that I'm no longer alive.

If I cry in front of you, read the lines,
Etched on my face, where the truth aligns.
The vulnerability, a language unsaid,
In the tears, emotions intricately spread.

If I cry in front of you, it's the surrender,

A confession that my strength is slender.
In the cascade of tears, a silent scream,
A plea for solace, for a shattered dream.

If I cry in front of you, touch the sorrow,
The rawness of pain, a darkened tomorrow.
In the vulnerability, find a fragment of me,
A soul laid bare, yearning to be free.

If I cry in front of you, bear witness to
The fragments of a spirit, tried and true.
In the tears, find the strength to mend,
For when I cry, my limits transcend.

Don't Give Me Silence

Don't give me silence, a void so deep,
Where words unspoken in shadows creep.
In the hush, hear the echoes of despair,
And say you care, beyond the vacant air.

Don't give me silence, a frigid stare,
In the quiet, emotions left threadbare.
Speak with the warmth of a tender flame,
Show me love, not just in your name.

Don't give me silence, a cavernous space,
Where echoes of longing can't find a trace.
Let your words be the balm to my wounds,
A melody that in my heart resounds.

Don't give me silence, an empty plea,
A void that speaks of apathy.
Actions louder than the quiet air,
Prove you care, beyond the vacant stare.

Don't give me silence, a chasm wide,
Let your love be a constant tide.
In the stillness, let empathy reside,
Speak with your heart, not just your pride.

Don't give me silence, a cruel jest,

In the quiet, let emotions be expressed.
Care not just in absence but presence true,
A symphony of words, a love that grew.

Don't give me silence, a deafening sound,
In the quiet, let compassion abound.
Show me you care with words that bind,
A love that echoes, true and kind.

Solitude's Embrace

In solitude's embrace, I build my wall,
A fortress of silence, a shield to install.
Against the yearning, against the fray,
I shut down, push everyone away.

The heart, a reluctant prisoner confined,
In the sanctuary of my mind.
Yet beneath the surface, a silent plea,
Yearning for connection, for a soul to see.

Fingers trace the scars, the walls I've made,
A self-imposed exile, in shadows laid.
Eyes that reflect the ache, the inner war,
As I push away, crave a little more.

In the echo of solitude, emotions entwine,
A dance of contradiction, a painful sign.
Yearning for closeness, yet afraid to stay,
I shut down, push everyone away.

A paradox in whispers, a silent scream,
A soul yearning for love, lost in the extreme.
The paradox of distance, the fear to stay,
In shutting down, love's price to pay.

In the empty spaces, where echoes linger,

A heart's rebellion, a trembling quiver.
Yet the yearning persists, an unspoken plea,
To break the cycle, to set emotions free.

Shutting down, an instinctive art,
Yet within the silence, beats a fragile heart.
Pushing away, a defensive play,
Yet deep down, I long to let you stay.

The Transformation

Beneath the weight of wounds, a transformation brews,
A metamorphosis, a soul that once knew.
Repeated hurts, like relentless waves,
Carve new contours, shape the one who braves.

The mirror reflects a stranger's gaze,
Eyes that have weathered countless maze.
Bearing the scars of battles unseen,
A transformed self, no longer serene.

The heart, once tender, now wears a guise,
A protective armor, a shield that implies.
Each hurt, a chisel on the sculpture of the soul,
Crafting a version, unfamiliar, yet whole.

In the echoes of pain, a voice distorts,
Whispers of trust, the heart contorts.
Betrayals etch lines upon the face,
A metamorphosis in the heart's embrace.

The laughter, once vibrant, now muted by scars,
A symphony of resilience beneath the stars.
Wounds that echo through the passage of time,
Turned into someone I don't recognize.

Yet within the shadows, a flicker remains,

A glimmer of hope, despite the stains.
For in the crucible of pain and strife,
A rebirth occurs, a rediscovery of life.

So, let the scars tell a tale untold,
Of a heart transformed, of a spirit bold.
In the crucible of hurt, emerges a prize,
A resilient self, with newfound eyes.

The Silent Refuge

Silence becomes my refuge, my shield,
A fortress built when emotions yield.
When wounds are fresh, when feelings bruise,
I retreat within, a defense to choose.

The echoes of past hurts still linger,
A haunting melody, a silent singer.
The pain, a familiar, unwelcome guest,
Compels me to withdraw, to seek rest.

In the silence, I fold into myself,
A cocoon of solitude, a book on a shelf.
A refuge from the storm of hurt,
Yet within, a tempest, a pain assert.

Each silent moment, a muted cry,
A dam of emotions, a tear-stained sky.
The words unspoken weigh heavy, like lead,
A history of abuse, a shadow I tread.

I long to articulate the ache, the sting,
But silence wraps around me like a wing.
A self-protective instinct, a learned art,
To guard the fragments of a battered heart.

Yet, within the silence, a longing resides,

For understanding, for healing tides.
The silence, a double-edged sword,
A way to cope, yet a connection ignored.

In the quiet, emotions take their toll,
A complex dance, a wounded soul.
I yearn for the strength to break free,
From the silence that envelopes me.

For in the breaking of the hush, a chance,
To heal, to grow, to reclaim my stance.
To find a voice amid the silent night,
And emerge from the shadows into the light.

The Healer

In the wreckage of a fragile soul,
I extend my hands, a desperate goal.
To mend the fractures, to soothe the ache,
To fix someone breaking, for their sake.

A history of scars, etched deep within,
Yet in my heart, a determination to begin.
To be the healer, the mender of wounds,
To dispel the shadows, unveil the cocoons.

But with each attempt to fix, I find,
A labyrinth of pain, a complex bind.
Their broken pieces, sharp and frail,
Yet I persist, despite the emotional gale.

In the mirror of their eyes, I see,
Reflections of a past that won't set free.
A history of abuse, a haunting past,
Yet I reach out, my compassion cast.

The weight of their burdens, a heavy load,
Yet I stand resilient, on this broken road.
To fix someone breaking, a daunting feat,
Yet love compels, and compassion beats.

A torrent of emotions, a tumultuous sea,

As I try to fix what no one else can see.
In their brokenness, I find my strength,
A determination that spans the length.

Yet within this struggle, I feel the strain,
The echoes of my own history, the past's refrain.
A woman with scars, trying to mend,
A cycle of healing that has no end.

To fix someone breaking, a selfless quest,
Yet, in their healing, I find unrest.
For in my efforts to mend their core,
I'm reminded of wounds I can't ignore.

In the journey to heal another's plight,
I navigate the currents of my own fight.
To fix someone breaking, I strive to be,
A beacon of hope, a lifeline at sea.

Worthless

She holds the wisdom of love within,
A tender heart with scars too thin.
Knowing the language, the gentle art,
Yet feeling unworthy, torn apart.

In the tapestry of her soul, love's design,
Woven with threads of a troubled line.
A history of shadows, a haunting past,
Leaves her feeling undeserving, a love miscast.

She understands the dance, the give and take,
Yet within herself, doubts quake.
A survivor of storms, of wounds so deep,
Feels unworthy of the love she keeps.

In the mirror's gaze, she sees the flaws,
Wounds that whisper, love withdraws.
Her heart knows how to embrace the light,
Yet in her own worthiness, she finds a fight.

A history of abuse, a silent scar,
Leaves her questioning who you are.
To love with depth, to understand,
Yet feeling unworthy, like shifting sand.

The echoes of past hurts, a haunting song,

In her heart, a doubt that lingers long.
She offers love with hands unsure,
Yet feels undeserving, love's allure.

She longs to break free from the chains,
To embrace the love that gently reigns.
A contradiction in the depths she feels,
Knowing how to love, yet doubt reveals.

In the struggle to reconcile her worth,
She tends love's garden, yet fears its dearth.
A woman with a heart so pure,
Yet feeling unworthy, love's obscure.

She's a paradox of strength and doubt,
In her heart, love's flame flickers, a muted shout.
Knowing the language, the tender dove,
Yet feeling unworthy of the love.

How Many Times

How many times can the same thing break your heart,
A relentless echo, a tear-stained start?
The fractures run deep, like rivers in the night,
A woman with a history, a silent fight.

How many times can the same thing break your heart,
In the echoes of pain, where emotions depart?
A history of scars, etched on her soul,
Each wound a reminder, a toll.

How many times can the same thing break your heart,
A cycle of hurt, a cruel art?
She weaves resilience from threads so thin,
Yet the repetition leaves her spirit thin.

How many times can the same thing break your heart,
A question that lingers, tearing apart?
In the silence of suffering, a woman stands,
A mosaic of heartbreak held in her hands.

How many times can the same thing break your heart,
A vulnerability, a fragmented art?
Yet within her eyes, a spark remains,
A strength that withstands recurring pains.

How many times can the same thing break your heart,

A woman's tale, a relentless chart?
In the struggle to heal, to redefine,
She finds the courage, the strength to shine.

How many times can the same thing break your heart,
In the echoes of hurt, a resilient start?
She rises again, from the ashes of pain,
A woman with scars, yet not in vain.

How many times can the same thing break your heart,
A testament to strength, an emotional art?
For in the breaking, in the tears that fall,
She finds the power to rise, to stand tall.

Entangled

In the tapestry of my heart, a constant thread,
A lingering emotion, where feelings are bred.
For that one person, a presence unseen,
In the spaces between, where memories convene.

A history of scars, etched on my soul,
Yet for them, a tenderness I can't control.
In the quiet corners, where emotions reside,
A love that lingers, a flame undenied.

Despite the shadows, the darkness I've known,
For that one person, my heart has grown.
A vulnerability, a bittersweet taste,
A love that time nor distance can erase.

In the echo of their name, my heart quickens pace,
A familiar rhythm, an enduring embrace.
Feelings entwined, like vines that climb,
A love that defies the constraints of time.

The history of abuse, a heavy weight,
Yet for them, my heart won't abate.
In the depth of my soul, a flicker remains,
A love that endures, despite the pains.

It makes me feel like a vulnerable bloom,

In the garden of love, where emotions loom.
For that one person, my heart still yearns,
A flame that within the heart burns.

In the dance of emotions, a silent song,
For that one person, my heart still longs.
A connection unbroken, a love profound,
In the recesses of my heart, forever unbound.

The Begger

In the quiet echoes of my heart's plea,
I stand before you, vulnerable, you see.
A history of scars, etched upon my soul,
Yet here I am, bearing love's heavy toll.

I beg you, with eyes that have weathered storms,
To see the love within, where passion forms.
In the tapestry of my vulnerability,
A woman pleads, yearning for sincerity.

Feelings entwined, a delicate dance,
Yet I fear rejection, a second chance.
In the shadowed corners of my history,
I beg you, love me, set my heart free.

The weight of my past, a burden to bear,
Yet for your love, I'm willing to dare.
Beneath the scars, a heart that believes,
In the power of love that never deceives.

I beg you, with whispers that tremble,
To look beyond the wounds, to disassemble
The walls I've built, the protective veneer,
And see the love that's sincere.

In the echoes of pain, where my voice wavers,

I beg you, my love, be my life-saver.
To mend the fractures, to soothe the ache,
And in your love, a refuge to make.

I stand before you, heart laid bare,
Begging for love, in the open air.
In the depth of my eyes, a plea,
To love me, to heal me, endlessly.

For in this moment, vulnerability reigns,
A woman's heart, love sustains.
I beg you, with a soul that yearns,
To love me, as my wounded heart learns.

Respect Me

With a heart that's weathered storms untold,
I stand before you, my spirit bold.
In the echoes of past wounds, I make my plea,
Begging you to see, to respect the woman in me.

A history of scars etched on my skin,
Yet within me, a strength from deep within.
I beg you, with eyes that have shed countless tears,
To honor my essence, allay my fears.

In the shadows where my history weaves,
I plead for respect, a soul that grieves.
The weight of past disrespect, a heavy chain,
I beg you to break it, release the pain.

Feelings entwined with the fabric of time,
Yet, respect is the rhythm, the sweetest rhyme.
In the tapestry of emotions that I bear,
I beg you, treat my heart with gentle care.

I beg you to listen to my silent cries,
To see the strength in my tear-stained eyes.
In the history of hurt, where my soul's been tested,
I beg for respect, to feel protected.

In the dance of vulnerability, where I stand,

I beg you to hold my trembling hand.
To understand the scars that define,
And in your respect, let my spirit shine.

I beg you, with a voice that trembles but is clear,
To respect the woman standing here.
In the echoes of pain, where my voice resounds,
I beg for respect that knows no bounds.

For in the quiet plea of a woman's heart,
Respect is the healing, the essential part.
I beg you to see, to truly see,
And in respecting me, set my spirit free.

Reflection

In the mirror of actions, the truth unfolds,
Reflections of feelings, tales untold.
For how someone treats you, an intimate art,
A canvas painted with the colors of the heart.

In the silence of gestures, emotions reveal,
A love sincere or a love that steals.
The echoes of words, the spaces between,
Speak louder than the surface sheen.

In the dance of connection, a subtle sway,
The way they treat you, what they convey.
For the heart leaves footprints in every act,
A symphony of feelings, a subtle impact.

The touch, a language, skin to skin,
Tells a story of the love within.
Or perhaps, the absence, the cold retreat,
A silent message, a love discreet.

In the moments shared, in glances exchanged,
The way they treat you, feelings arranged.
The kindness, a reflection of affection,
Or the neglect, a subtle rejection.

In the poetry of actions, emotions inscribe,

The truth of feelings, no need to bribe.
For how someone treats you, an open door,
To the depths of their love, or something more.

So read the script in every gaze,
The tenderness or the love ablaze.
For how someone treats you, a revelation,
Of the emotions that shape their foundation.

In the art of existence, emotions play,
A role in every word and gesture displayed.
In the tapestry of feelings, woven true,
How they treat you, a glimpse into their view.

You Can't Fix Me

In the wreckage of my spirit, shattered and worn,
You were the architect of a love forlorn.
Through the cracks in my heart, pain does seep,
A love that promised, only to leave me weep.

You, the sculptor of my deepest despair,
Can't be the one to mend, to repair.
For in breaking me, you held the chisel,
Carved wounds so deep, left me brittle.

Your hands that once promised solace and care,
Now leave me drowning in a sea of despair.
In the ruins of trust, a darkness looms,
A love once vibrant, now a silent tomb.

I'm the canvas painted with hues of your deceit,
A masterpiece of agony, incomplete.
You, the architect of my own demise,
Can't be the healer of my tear-stained cries.

For the hands that broke the fragile thread,
Can't be the ones to sew me whole instead.
In the wreckage you crafted, where pain resides,
You can't be the one to heal the tides.

Each shattered piece, a testament to your art,

A symphony of brokenness, tearing me apart.
Your touch, once soothing, now a poison kiss,
A love that crumbled, a blissful abyss.

In the echo of my heartache, a silent plea,
You can't be the one to set me free.
For the hands that break, in their grip so tight,
Can't be the ones to mend the fractured light.

As I gather the fragments, piece by piece,
In the mosaic of healing, a soul's release.
Your touch, a memory etched in pain,
A love dismantled, never to regain.

So let the tears fall, in the quiet night,
For a love that crumbled, a fading light.
In the ruins of us, a phoenix may rise,
But you can't be the one to mend my skies.

Desolation

Beneath the weight of words that cut like knives,
I retreat into the solace where the music thrives.
A melody to drown the echoes of my despair,
A symphony to silence the hurt I bear.

In the cadence of songs, I find my escape,
A refuge where emotions take on a different shape.
The lyrics become a shield, a fortress strong,
Against the memories of all that went wrong.

The volume rises, a crescendo of disguise,
Drowning out the echoes of silent cries.
A desperate attempt to escape the pain,
In the rhythm of songs, where emotions wane.

The beats become my heartbeat, steady and sure,
A pulse that resonates, a painless allure.
For in the lyrics, I find a voice,
A sanctuary where I make my choice.

To turn up the music, to drown out the noise,
The haunting whispers of cruel decoys.
The bass reverberates, a calming drum,
A retreat from the battles, a refuge to become numb.

Yet behind the lyrics, the truth remains,

A heart that's fractured, bound in chains.
In the melodies, I bury my fears,
A facade to conceal the cascade of tears.

The crescendo of songs can't heal the scars,
But for a moment, I escape the bars.
The playlist becomes my silent plea,
To forget the pain, to just be free.

So, in the symphony, I find my peace,
A temporary respite, a fleeting release.
But when the music fades, reality returns,
A broken heart in silence, for the healing yearns.

Drowning

Beyond the curtain of my painted smile,
I labor to exude joy, but all the while,
Beneath the surface, a fractured soul,
A performance of happiness, a draining role.

In the echoes of laughter, a hollow sound,
A facade constructed, a mask tightly wound.
The scars, unseen, beneath the veneer,
A stage where the script is not entirely clear.

The spotlight on happiness, a relentless blaze,
Yet in the shadows, where exhaustion lays.
Each smile, a labor, a wearisome feat,
A charade of joy, where true feelings retreat.

To paint on my face a radiant gleam,
Is to deny the scars that lie between.
The echoes of abuse, the relentless strife,
Hidden behind a semblance of a happy life.

Each moment of mirth is a silent plea,
To drown the echoes of what used to be.
Yet, in the masquerade, a soul wears thin,
A heart working hard, struggling to begin.

The applause of happiness, a bitter cheer,

A script rehearsed, year after year.
A performance to convince, a draining art,
To mend the fragments of a broken heart.

In the echo of laughter, a silent cry,
A wish for authenticity, to soar, to fly.
Yet the weight of pretense, a heavy cloak,
Drains the spirit, as happiness I invoke.

So, behind the painted smile, tears may flow,
A river of sorrow, a hidden undertow.
For the effort to feel happy, a relentless quest,
Leaves a heart weary, in need of rest.

The Silent Thief

Beneath the weight of words that cut like knives,
I carry the burden of a fractured life.
From verbal slights to fists that bruise,
A shattered spirit, caught in the abuse.

Doubt creeps in like a silent thief,
Stealing the remnants of my belief.
A whispering echo, relentless and cold,
Declaring I'm damaged, a story untold.

In the mirror, I see the broken reflection,
A soul shackled by self-rejection.
Emotional wounds, an internal storm,
A belief I'm destined for endless scorn.

The bruises may fade, but the ache within,
A constant reminder of where I've been.
Words, like poison, seep into my core,
Whispering I'm worthless, forevermore.

Doubt, a shadow that never retreats,
In the quiet moments, its presence repeats.
I question my worth, my purpose, my fate,
A broken record, a relentless debate.

Drained by the doubt that clouds my mind,

A self-fulfilling prophecy, unkind.
I carry the weight of a damaged soul,
A heart convinced it will never be whole.

Yet within the fractures, a flicker remains,
A spark of strength that endures the chains.
For despite the doubt, the self-deprecating song,
I am resilient, and I can be strong.

In the symphony of doubt, a silent cry,
A plea for healing, a desperate try.
To break free from the chains that bind,
And discover the worth within my mind.

For I am more than the bruises and doubt,
A spirit unbroken, seeking a way out.
In the intensity of struggle, I find a light,
A glimmer of hope in the darkest night.

Don't Lie to Me

Don't lie to me, I've danced in deceit's embrace,
A history of falsehoods etched on my heart's surface.
Words, once sweet, now echo with a bitter sting,
In the symphony of lies, where trust took wing.

Don't lie to me, for I've weathered the storm,
In the labyrinth of deception, my heart was torn.
Each promise shattered, a fractured vow,
I've seen the wreckage; I know it now.

Don't lie to me, for the scars run deep,
A tapestry of pain, where secrets seep.
I question each truth, each whispered word,
For in the echoes of lies, my trust was blurred.

Don't lie to me, I carry the weight,
Of a love betrayed, a twisted fate.
The burden of doubt, a relentless weight,
In the cycle of lies, my heart stagnates.

Don't lie to me, for the truth seems unclear,
A specter of distrust, always near.
The wounds of the past bleed into today,
A heart guarded, a price to pay.

Don't lie to me, for I've seen love's demise,

In the betrayal of truth, where hope lies.
I build walls with every unspoken lie,
A fortress of doubt, reaching the sky.

Don't lie to me, in the dance of connection,
A heart wounded, seeking affection.
Yet every whisper of love, every gentle plea,
Is met with skepticism, the ghost of past agony.

Don't lie to me, for the trust is frail,
A relentless doubt, an emotional gale.
In the echo of lies, my heart's plea,
To break free from the cycle, to just believe.

Forsaken

In the dance of fleeting moments, he stood,
A whisper of forever, misunderstood.
His eyes, like stars, spoke of dreams untold,
Yet, in my haste, their stories I'd withhold.

He painted tomorrows with strokes so divine,
A masterpiece of love, a tapestry to entwine.
But I, a wanderer in the shadows of doubt,
Brushed off his plea, cast forever out.

Regret now lingers, a bittersweet song,
A melody of chances lost, moments gone wrong.
For in the echo of his unspoken vow,
I find myself yearning for what's lost now.

The hands of time, relentless in their flight,
Carry the weight of an unspoken goodbye.
Oh, how I wish to turn back the tide,
Embrace the forever I pushed aside.

In the silence, echoes the ache of remorse,
A dance with destiny, a divergent course.
He offered eternity, a love so sincere,
Yet, I let it slip through, my greatest fear.

Now, in solitude, I bear the cost,

Of a love forsaken, of forever lost.
A lesson learned in the echoes of regret,
A plea for a second chance, I'll never forget.

My Worth

Constantly I strive to prove my worth,
A soul fractured, bound to the earth.
In the echoes of abuse, a haunting refrain,
A heart convinced it's destined for pain.

I must articulate, set the rules clear,
A damaged spirit filled with fear.
Words that once stung, etched on my soul,
I strive to rise, to reclaim control.

I whisper to the wind, the plea unsaid,
A heart battered, a spirit unwed.
For every gesture, every touch bestowed,
I must justify, prove my worth, forebode.

In the mirror, a reflection of broken dreams,
A mosaic of scars, more than it seems.
I bear the weight of my battered past,
A narrative written, a die long cast.

Tell me I matter, my worth to define,
In the chaos of doubt, where shadows align.
Yet the echoes persist, a relentless sound,
A heart convinced it's destined to drown.

I paint on a smile, a veneer so thin,

A facade to conceal the pain within.
To prove I'm worth love, respect, and care,
A constant battle, a soul laid bare.

My voice trembles as I set the decree,
A plea for kindness, for eyes to see,
That beneath the damage, the fractured clay,
A spirit endures, seeking a brighter day.

In the dance of proving, a relentless chore,
A heart yearns for love, for something more.
Yet the scars, like chains, a binding tether,
An echo of pain that lasts forever.

I navigate the darkness, the shadows cast,
A journey to prove that I will last.
In the symphony of struggle, my soul's decree,
To rise from the ashes, to break free.

Deception

Deceptive whispers veiled in affection's guise,
I believed your words, swallowed your lies.
In the shadows of promises, deceit took flight,
A heart betrayed, a soul eclipsed in night.

Actions, louder than the sweetest verse,
Left me broken, a love immersed.
I mistook cruelty for love's embrace,
A painful truth, a bitter taste.

Your touch, once tender, now a cruel jest,
A veil of care concealing the unrest.
I believed the facade, the act you portrayed,
Yet beneath the surface, love decayed.

I saw care in your eyes, or so it seemed,
Yet actions spoke louder than I'd dreamed.
A painful revelation, a heart deceived,
In the shattered fragments, love retrieved.

The echoes of abuse, a haunting score,
A love that crumbled, a soul left sore.
I believed in the caring, the mirage you portrayed,
Yet actions proved love was betrayed.

Don't Waste My Time

Listen, love, I've danced in shadows deep,
Where pain and heartache, their secrets keep.
Broken and shattered, I've tread the night,
A mosaic of wounds, each one a fight.

Don't waste my time if you fear the fray,
For my heart's been wounded, led astray.
In the echoes of heartbreak, I find my voice,
A survivor's anthem, a steadfast choice.

I've mended the fragments, stitched the pain,
A broken soul seeking solace in the rain.
If you can't handle the scars I bear,
Don't waste my time with a love that's rare.

I've been through the storms, a tempest's roar,
In the wreckage, I found strength to explore.
But if you're not ready for a damaged heart,
Don't waste my time with a false start.

I need extra attention, a patient hand,
Someone willing to understand.
If you can't embrace the shadows I've known,
Don't waste my time, just let me be alone.

I've fought battles in the darkened alleys,

A warrior's spirit, battered and calloused.
If you can't hold the weight of my past,
Don't waste my time, it's a truth steadfast.

So, love, if you're not ready for the climb,
If damaged hearts make you fear the time,
Don't waste my moments with a hesitant rhyme,
I'm mending myself, it's a journey sublime.

Self-Sabotage

In shadows cast by a broken dawn,
A soul once vibrant, now withdrawn.
Bearing scars that silently weep,
A tale of torment, buried deep.

She danced with demons, embraced the pain,
A toxic waltz, a cruel refrain.
Bruised petals of a fragile rose,
In the garden where sorrow grows.

Emotional tempests, storms unseen,
Echoes of a love, once serene.
Whispers linger, haunting the air,
A tortured heart, burdened with despair.

In the mirror, she seeks her own gaze,
Reflection warped in a shattered maze.
A canvas painted with hues of despair,
Self-sabotage tangled in her hair.

Her worth obscured in the ashes of doubt,
A flame flickering, struggling to sprout.
Yet, within the core, resilience stirs,
A silent anthem, as hope recurs.

A phoenix rising from ashes charred,

Each scar a testament, each wound, a bard.
Through the wreckage, she finds her way,
Unraveling night to welcome the day.

Fingers tracing the jagged lines,
Unveiling strength that silently shines.
No longer captive to a ghostly past,
She forges a future, free at last.

A metamorphosis, a rebirth,
She reclaims the fragments, her own self-worth.
In the crucible of pain, she finds her voice,
A symphony of healing, a resilient choice.

Control

In the silence of scars, a tale unfolds,
A spirit battered, a story untold.
Physical echoes, emotional bruise,
A heart once whole, now tethered to abuse.

Control, a lifeline in a world askew,
A desperate grasp, a safety cue.
Fingers clenched, knuckles turned to white,
Yearning for order in the chaos of night.

Haunted by shadows, a turbulent past,
Every moment a battle, each breath the last.
Yet, in the yearning for a grasp too tight,
Dances the fragility of a wounded light.

Within the chaos, a whisper of grace,
Yearning for solace in the tumultuous space.
Through the tremors of a soul unrest,
A journey unfolds, a healing quest.

In the crucible of control, emotions surge,
A desperate plea, a silent urge.
Yet, in surrender, strength is found,
A resilient spirit, breaking through the ground.

For every fracture, a chance to mend,

In the fragments, a story to transcend.
Through the storm of yearning, a soul takes flight,
From the ashes of control, emerges the light.

A Heartfelt Stare

In the quiet moments when shadows fade,
I yearn for a gaze, a promise unmade.
To be seen with eyes that truly perceive,
A worth beyond measure, where doubts can't deceive.

In the mirror's reflection, I seek to find,
A reflection of worth, a soul intertwined.
I long for a glance that speaks without words,
Affirming my value, like the sweetest of chords.

To be held in regard, a treasure untold,
A story of worth in every gaze that unfolds.
Not for the masks I wear, but for what lies within,
A recognition of value, where love can begin.

Oh, to be worthy of all that they see,
A canvas of dreams, a symphony free.
In the tapestry of glances, may I find,
A recognition that echoes, "she's worth every kind."

For in the simplicity of a heartfelt stare,
Lies the affirmation, the answer to prayer.
To be valued completely, with no need for proof,
Oh, to be seen as worth every ounce of truth.

To the Ones Who Hold My Heart So Dear

To the ones who hold my heart so dear,
I pen a verse, sincere and clear.
In the canvas of life, I failed to see,
The importance of tending to me.

For every tear, I couldn't keep at bay,
I apologize for the cloudy day.
In neglecting myself, I failed you too,
A truth I now confront, overdue.

The burdens I carried, heavy and wide,
Impacted the moments we could've enjoyed.
I didn't nurture my flame, now dim,
Forgive me, my loves, for the shadows within.

You deserved a caregiver robust and whole,
A pillar of strength, a nurturing soul.
In my quest for your joy, I lost a part,
A lesson learned, breaking my heart.

Yet, let this apology weave a new start,
A promise to mend and heal every part.
For in caring for me, I'll better care for you,
A journey of love, sincere and true.

Toxic Bonds

To those who watched me in silent strife,
A whispered apology, a bittersweet life.
In toxic bonds, I lost my way,
Failed to seek the light of a brighter day.

I wore a mask, a facade so strong,
Yet, inside, a symphony of things went wrong.
Shoulders burdened, heart heavy like lead,
I apologize for the words left unsaid.

To those who wished to lend a hand,
I pushed away, couldn't understand.
A prisoner in silence, a self-made cell,
Forgive me, dear ones, for I failed to tell.

The weight I carried, a solitary load,
In silence, I wandered, a lonesome road.
For not reaching out when the shadows fell,
I apologize; my silence spoke too well.

Now, as I mend, I learn to confide,
In asking for help, humility as my guide.
To those who care, I open my heart,
A belated plea for a fresh start.

Settling

Dear self, in the mirror's gaze I see,
A reflection of apologies, whispered to me.
In the echoes of toxic whispers and lies,
I apologize for the tears in your eyes.

I settled for less, when you deserved more,
In the shadows of compromise, your spirit wore.
For every compromise, each hushed plea,
I'm sorry, dear self, for not setting you free.

In the maze of toxicity, a twisted dance,
I let you settle, gave toxicity a chance.
For every compromise, a silent surrender,
Forgive me, dear self, for the wounds so tender.

I should have sought love, not a counterfeit,
A genuine connection, not a toxic fit.
In settling for less, I dimmed your light,
I apologize, dear self, for the endless night.

Yet, from the ruins, a strength emerges clear,
A promise to self, to hold you near.
In the apology, a pledge to rise above,
To rediscover self, and rekindle self-love.

Forgive the Doubt

To the echoes within, my soul's gentle plea,
Forgive me, dear self, for I failed to see.
In the tapestry of doubts, woven so clever,
I apologize for believing I didn't deserve better.

I accepted morsels, crumbs of affection,
Questioned my worth in a distorted reflection.
In the shadows of doubt, where silence resides,
I apologize for the dreams cast aside.

Believing I was less, when I'm made of stars,
Forgive me, dear self, for these self-imposed bars.
In the canvas of insecurity, painted so bold,
I apologize for the stories left untold.

I doubted the love that resides within,
A sacred flame, a sanctuary to begin.
Forgiveness, I seek, for the times I faltered,
For the belief that I, too, could be unaltered.

Now, in the mirror, I see strength anew,
A journey unfolding, a self-love so true.
Forgive me, dear self, as I rise above,
Embracing the worthiness of this boundless love.

Deeply Flawed

In the quiet chambers of my own mind,
I seek forgiveness, a solace to find.
For years I carried a heavy load,
Believing I was the problem, a tale untold.

In the maze of self-blame, shadows danced,
A relentless cycle, a trance enhanced.
Forgive me, dear self, for the pain I caused,
For believing I was deeply flawed.

I draped myself in guilt's heavy cloak,
Blinded by whispers, a self-inflicted joke.
For every tear shed in the dark,
I beg for forgiveness, a genuine spark.

I mistook clouds for a storm within,
Lost in a narrative where I couldn't win.
For doubting the essence of who I am,
Forgive me, dear self, for the self-inflicted harm.

Now, in the mirror, I seek your eyes,
To mend the wounds, where forgiveness lies.
A journey unfolds, a path to grace,
Forgiving myself, embracing the embrace.

Guarded

To the self yet unseen, my future reflection,
In the fortress of walls, a silent protection.
Forgive me, dear self, for the barriers tall,
Erected in shadows, guarding against the fall.

In the aftermath of trauma's cruel dance,
Walls rose, an unintended defense.
A shield against echoes of a haunting past,
A barricade built to make love last.

To the one who loves me next, a plea,
Through the barricades, my heart can't see.
Apologies for the walls that stand,
Built by the touch of a hurtful hand.

A fortress I crafted, brick by brick,
To shield against wounds, the echoes thick.
Forgive me, dear one, for the guarded gate,
For the hesitations, the love delayed.

In the garden of love, let forgiveness bloom,
As we dismantle walls, dispel the gloom.
A promise to trust, to let love in,
Apologies for the battles we may begin.

Dear future self, a vow to break free,

From the walls that encase, imprison me.
To the one who loves, a pledge to unfold,
A story of healing, a love to be told.

Remorse

In the quiet corridors of remorse, I tread,
A symphony of apologies, my heart has said.
I'm sorry for the walls that I built so high,
For not allowing your love to reach the sky.

In the echo of silence, my regrets resound,
A dance of shadows, where love was bound.
I pushed you away, in fear's disguise,
An apologetic tear in regretful eyes.

I'm sorry for the moments I turned and fled,
Afraid of the love that could have been spread.
The warmth you offered, I couldn't receive,
A prisoner of doubts, I struggled to believe.

In the garden of affection, I closed the gate,
Denied the blossoms of a love so great.
I see now the beauty I was blind to see,
And in my heart, aching, I set you free.

The tapestry of time weaves a tale,
Of apologies whispered in the night's frail.
I long to rewind and undo the wrong,
To embrace the love that was strong.

I'm sorry for the scars that my fear may leave,

For the moments of doubt that I failed to relieve.
In the echoes of remorse, a sincere plea,
Forgive me for not letting you love me.

A Quiet Goodbye

In the hush of silence, emotions concealed,
Shutting down, a fortress tightly sealed.
A quiet storm, brewing within,
The pain of restraint, the battle to win.

For in the stillness, a tempest grows,
A hurricane of feelings that no one knows.
Beneath the surface, emotions erupt,
Yet, shutting down is the bitterest cup.

The explosion may be fiery, fierce, and loud,
But shutting down, a tempest in a shroud.
Words unspoken, wounds unseen,
A silent war where hearts convene.

The aftermath of silence, a lingering scar,
A canyon of distance, stretching far.
Blowing up may burn, but it clears the air,
Shutting down, a weight too heavy to bear.

So, let emotions flow, like a raging tide,
In the chaos, love and pain coincide.
For shutting down, in its muted cry,
Is a storm within, a quiet goodbye.

I Think of You Often

I think of you often, in the quiet of the night,
A best friend's echo, wrapped in soft moonlight.
Our laughter and secrets, a cherished blend,
Yet, in the silence, I yearn for more, my old friend.

I think of you often, as the stars align,
Moments of intimacy, frozen in time.
You craved forever, a commitment so deep,
But I hesitated, in promises I couldn't keep.

I think of you often, in the whispers of the past,
A love unspoken, destined not to last.
You wanted more than friendship, a truth sincere,
Yet, my heart hesitated, fueled by fear.

I think of you often, in the shadows we cast,
A dance of what-ifs, a love unsurpassed.
In those moments shared, where emotions unfurled,
I ponder what could have been, in a different world.

I think of you often, and the choice I made,
To hold back the love that could not evade.
You wanted forever, a commitment, a vow,
But I couldn't say yes, not then, but now...

I think of you often, with a bittersweet smile,

H. WALDON

Regret and longing, a complicated mile.
In the tapestry of memories that we weave,
I think of you often, in the love I couldn't retrieve.

Masterpiece Undone

You broke me, like shattered glass on cold ground,
You broke me, the silence of heartache, profound.
You broke me, in the echoes of a love unsaid,
You broke me, a symphony of tears I've shed.

You broke me, with words left unspoken,
You broke me, a fragile spirit, now broken.
You broke me, like promises lost in the wind,
You broke me, and the wounds lie within.

You broke me, in the chapters left unwritten,
You broke me, the pieces scattered, smitten.
You broke me, like a fragile porcelain dream,
You broke me, and nothing's as it seems.

You broke me, a masterpiece undone,
You broke me, in the setting of the sun.
You broke me, in the dance of what was meant to be,
You broke me, and now I'm just debris.

If We Never Met

I almost wish we never met,
You caused me stress, a heavy debt.
In the shadows, I crumbled down,
You slowly broke me, piece by piece, I found.

I almost wish we never met,
A constant battle, a soul beset.
Feelings of worthiness, torn and frayed,
In the echoes of your actions, my spirit swayed.

I almost wish we never met,
A narrative of heartache, hard to forget.
Yet, through the pain, a resilience grew,
A strength within, a breakthrough.

I almost wish we never met,
A sentiment of regret, I can't forget.
Yet, in the wreckage, a truth unfolds,
I am more than the story your presence holds.

I almost wish we never met, but just almost,
For in the crucible of pain, resilience boasts.
Through the fractures, strength found its way,
If we never met, I wouldn't be who I am today.

Almost

In the shadows of what might have been,
I ponder the tapestry, the threads so thin.
We danced on the edge of an elusive dream,
Yet, in my blindness, I chose a different scheme.

I think of everything we almost had,
A love untold, a story gone bad.
The echoes of laughter, the warmth we shared,
Now drowned in the silence, a love impaired.

In the corridors of memory, I trace,
A path of choices, a bittersweet embrace.
Regret and sadness, companions on this road,
Where the seeds of what we had failed to be sowed.

I think of a time when I could have had you,
But I chose a path where love withdrew.
Blinded by doubts and fears untold,
I embraced a story of regret, my heart's stronghold.

I didn't realize the path I chose,
A journey of sadness, where the river flows.
In the rearview mirror, I see the view,
Of a moment when I almost had you.

Always remembering when it was close,

The warmth, the love, the path we chose.
In the gallery of what-ifs, I hang my rue,
A portrait of when I almost had you.

Drained

In the quiet of my soul, a weary hush,
No more fight within, the embers' final blush.
The battles waged, a weary heart beseeched,
Drained and depleted, strength finally leached.

Once resilient, a spirit bold,
Now whispers surrender, the story untold.
The weight of burdens, an anchor's hold,
In the depths of weariness, my story unfolds.

I've fought the storms, faced the raging sea,
Yet, here I stand, no fight left in me.
The armor worn, now heavy and cold,
The echoes of struggle, a tale foretold.

Dreams once vivid, now a distant haze,
The fire within, a dwindling blaze.
No more resilience, no more might,
In the stillness, I surrender the fight.

I've climbed the mountains, faced the night,
But now I falter, no strength to ignite.
The battles have etched their marks so deep,
In this quiet surrender, my soul does weep.

No more fight left, the banners fall,

A weary heart, surrendering all.
In the silence, I find my reprieve,
No more fight left, yet still, I grieve.

If Only

If only I had said yes,
To the love that you offered, a gentle caress.
But I faltered, lost in my own fears,
Unsure of love's language, drowned in tears.

If only I had embraced,
The warmth of your love, the gentle grace.
But I hesitated, in shadows I hid,
Afraid of the love I couldn't forbid.

If only I had understood,
The depth of your love, the promise so good.
But I was lost in my own maze,
Unable to see through love's haze.

If only I had accepted,
The gift of your heart, so freely presented.
But I turned away, in doubt's embrace,
Unaware of love's gentle grace.

If only I had let you in,
To the depths of my soul, where love begins.
But I built walls, brick by brick,
Afraid to feel, afraid to pick.

If only I had seen,

The beauty of love, the places we'd been.
But I chose a path that led astray,
Leaving behind what could have stayed.

If only I had said yes,
To the love that could have healed, and blessed.
But now I yearn for what could have been,
In the silence, where echoes of regret begin.

Apologies

In the book of scars, where pain is inscribed,
Some wounds run deep, with shadows imbibed.
Apologies, like whispers, may softly plead,
Yet certain wounds persist, in silence they bleed.

No balm of sorry can mend the abyss,
Some wounds linger, a haunting kiss.
The echoes of regret may fill the air,
But certain wounds bear an enduring stare.

Apologies, fragile as a delicate sigh,
Seek refuge in the tear-stained sky.
Yet, in the heart's recesses, wounds may reside,
Defying the healing that mere words provide.

Some wounds carve valleys in the soul,
Apologies may echo, but can't make whole.
In the tapestry of pain, a tale unfolds,
Of wounds too deep, where forgiveness molds.

For there are scars that words can't erase,
A lingering ache, a sorrowful grace.
Apologies may dance, a delicate art,
Yet some wounds persist, etched on the heart.

Who Hurt You?

Who hurt you? My own expectations,
A silent torment, self-inflicted vexations.
In the realm of dreams, where illusions breed,
I found the pain, in my wants and need.

A dance with shadows, where desires entwine,
Who hurt you? My expectations, unkind.
I wove a tapestry of hopes untold,
Yet, in the unraveling, the bitter truth unfolds.

In the echo of yearning, a silent plea,
Who hurt you? The expectations within me.
I crafted a story, painted in hues,
Yet, expectations proved to be elusive clues.

Who hurt you? My illusions so grand,
In the castle of dreams built on shifting sand.
I sought solace in the arms of what could be,
Yet, expectations became chains, binding me.

In the reflection of shattered dreams,
Who hurt you? The expectations, it seems.
A self-imposed wound, a silent strife,
As I grapple with the expectations of life.

Who hurt you? My own silent cries,

In the quest for perfection, where discontent lies.
I release the expectations, let them fly,
For in their absence, true freedom lies.

Play Pretend

I pretend to be happy, a smile on my face,
A mask well-worn, in the crowded space.
Beneath the laughter, a quiet despair,
I pretend to be happy, but it's not always there.

I pretend to be happy, in the daylight's gleam,
A facade so convincing, a carefully crafted scheme.
Behind the brightness, shadows reside,
I pretend to be happy, my true self to hide.

I pretend to be happy, as the day unfolds,
A narrative scripted, with tales untold.
In the silence of night, when no one sees,
I pretend to be happy, but my heart disagrees.

I pretend to be happy, in the company of friends,
A charade of joy, a game that never ends.
Yet, in the solitude of my own company,
I pretend to be happy, but I long to be free.

I pretend to be happy, a role to play,
A script rehearsed, day after day.
In the theater of life, a lonely stage,
I pretend to be happy, in this self-made cage.

I pretend to be happy, but deep within,

A longing for authenticity, a desire to begin.
For behind the pretense, a truth I seek,
To break free from the act, to no longer speak.

Spite

In the shadowed corners where resentment breeds,
I stood beside you, tangled in spiteful deeds.
Your actions, like arrows, laced with disdain,
A tempest of spite, leaving scars, not rain.

A dance of shadows, fueled by disdain,
A toxic waltz, leaving a trail of pain.
Each gesture, a weapon, each word a blade,
In the garden of love, where poison was laid.

With every spiteful move, a poison dart,
Piercing the fabric of our shared heart.
A portrait painted in hues of regret,
A love entangled in a spiteful vignette.

In the quiet moments, where wounds fester,
I questioned the bond, a love's true tester.
Yet, I lingered, hoping for change,
In the midst of the spite, a love estranged.

The echoes of your spite, a haunting refrain,
A melody of hurt, a symphony of pain.
In the debris of love, where bitterness clings,
I sought solace in broken, shattered wings.

But in the end, I chose to break free,

From the chains of spite that bound you and me.
A farewell to shadows, a journey to light,
Escaping the clutches of perpetual spite.

In the healing echoes, a resilience found,
A love reclaimed, on higher ground.
A tale of lessons learned, in spite's cruel art,
A mended soul, a brand-new start.

Sweet Escape

In the haven of my thoughts, you find a place,
A sweet escape, a refuge, a warm embrace.
With every reverie, a tender flight,
Your presence, a beacon, in the gentle night.

Thoughts of you, like petals, soft and light,
A sweet escape, a dance in the moon's soft light.
In the realm of dreams, where fantasies weave,
Your essence, a melody, a love to believe.

Through the corridors of my mind, you roam,
A sweet escape, a sanctuary, my heart's own.
In the tapestry of thoughts, where emotions sway,
Your memory, a muse, in the quiet of the day.

In the symphony of whispers, where daydreams soar,
A sweet escape, a place I adore.
With thoughts of you, a tranquil spree,
A sweet escape, where my heart is free.

Not Surprised

Disappointed but not surprised, a familiar refrain,
In the ebb and flow of life, where expectations wane.
A sigh escapes, a fleeting glance,
As disappointment settles, in the dance.

Not surprised, for I've seen it before,
The fragile dreams shattered, on the floor.
In the tapestry of moments, where hope resides,
Disappointment lurks, in the shadows it hides.

I've tasted the bitterness, felt its sting,
Disappointed but not surprised, the echoes ring.
In the theater of life, where stories unfold,
Disappointment wears a cloak, its tale told.

The echoes of promises, now faded and worn,
Disappointed but not surprised, the truth is born.
In the silence of acceptance, a bitter pill,
Disappointment lingers, against my will.

Yet in the disappointment, a lesson lies,
A beacon of truth beneath the skies.
For in the dance of disappointment's guise,
Lies the strength to move forward, to rise.

Disappointed but not surprised, I stand tall,

For in disappointment, I find the call.
To embrace the journey, despite its disguise,
Disappointed but not surprised, I'll still rise.

Infinite Chances

In the realm of forgiveness, a heart so wide,
I've given chances, like the changing tide.
More than they deserved, in the dance of grace,
A mosaic of second chances, in life's embrace.

Each mistake, a brushstroke on the canvas of trust,
Yet, I've given chances, as if love is a must.
Beyond reason and rhyme, my heart extends,
A grace that transcends, even when it offends.

More chances than deserved, a generous rain,
Pouring down on wounds, washing away pain.
In the garden of forgiveness, where flowers bloom,
I've given chances, dispelling the gloom.

Yet, in the echoes of second and third,
A cautionary tale, a lesson learned.
For in the tapestry of chances, woven with care,
Sometimes, giving too much can lead to despair.

A heart so open, a spirit so kind,
Yet, giving chances, I've often find,
Can be a delicate balance, a dance on a thread,
Between the love that's given and the boundaries led.

In the symphony of chances, a melody played,

A choice to forgive, to let love cascade.
Yet, a mindful heart, a lesson to glean,
To give chances wisely, in the dance unforeseen.

Lost Within

You only liked the idea of me,
A fleeting mirage, a fantasy.
In the glow of illusions, where shadows blend,
The real me lost, in the echoes you send.

You liked the idea, a concept so sweet,
But the depth of my soul, you never did meet.
In the gallery of dreams, where fantasies spin,
The reality of my being, lost within.

You only liked the idea of my smile,
Yet, within the layers, thoughts reconcile.
A facade you embraced, a mask so thin,
The substance beneath, lost in the spin.

You liked the idea of my laughter's ring,
But the echoes of pain, you didn't bring.
In the silent moments, where truth resides,
The idea of me fades, reality abides.

You only liked the idea, a portrait so grand,
But the complexities within, you never planned.
In the tapestry of being, where truth should be,
You only liked the idea of me.

Yet, beyond the illusions, where shadows flee,

Exists the essence of me, waiting to be free.
In the dance of realities, where authenticity reigns,
You'll find the genuine me, breaking chains.

Delicate as Glass

You knew I was fragile, delicate as glass,
Yet you let me slip, a shattering trespass.
In the dance of trust, a precarious sway,
You knew I was fragile, but you dropped me anyway.

A whisper of vulnerability, a silent plea,
You held my heart, but let it be free.
In the fragile moments, where trust was built,
You let it fall, guiltless and guilt.

You knew I was fragile, like petals in the breeze,
Yet you released me, brought me to my knees.
In the mosaic of feelings, where emotions blend,
You let go, and I couldn't mend.

The fractures now echo, a silent cry,
In the wreckage of trust, where fragments lie.
You knew I was fragile, like porcelain lace,
Yet you dropped me, leaving an empty space.

In the aftermath, the pieces remain,
A testimony of love, lost in disdain.
You knew I was fragile, yet you chose to break,
The delicate bond, a choice to forsake.

In the Silence that Stretches

In the silence that stretches, an unspoken chasm,
Words unsaid, creating a quiet spasm.
The lack of communication, a void so deep,
A cavern of secrets where emotions sleep.

Through the echoes of unspoken desires,
A bridge of understanding, love requires.
The distance grows with each silent plea,
The lack of communication, a barrier to see.

In the spaces between unshared thoughts,
A relationship falters, its foundation caught.
The unspoken whispers, a deafening sound,
The lack of communication, love unbound.

The unspoken words, like stones in a stream,
A barrier rising, an emotional seam.
In the quietude, resentment takes root,
The lack of communication, a poisonous shoot.

A fracture widens with each unsaid word,
In the absence of dialogue, love's unheard.
Misunderstandings breed in the silence,
The lack of communication, a relational offense.

Yet, in the quiet, there's a chance to start,
To mend the rift, heal the wounded heart.
Communication's embrace, a bridge to build,
In the silence, love's potential fulfilled.

Just A Void

In the echoes of memory, a haunting refrain,
I'll never forget the sting of your disdain.
You made me feel like I was nothing, a void,
A silent ache, a love destroyed.

Your words, like arrows, pierced the air,
Reducing my worth, a soul left bare.
In the caverns of my heart, the wounds conceal,
The way you made me feel, so unreal.

I'll never forget the weight of your gaze,
A cold indifference, like a love ablaze.
In the tapestry of emotions, a thread unraveled,
The way you made me feel, forever traveled.

A whispered nothingness, etched in the air,
I carry the echoes, a burden to bear.
In the gallery of feelings, a portrait of pain,
I'll never forget the way you made me feel, disdain.

But in the echoes of hurt, resilience grows,
A strength untold, a spirit that knows.
I'll rise from the ashes of the wounds you dealt,
For the way you made me feel, won't be my heart's belt.

I Will Not Compete For You

I will not compete for you, in the race of desire,
For love cannot be won, like a trophy to acquire.
In the garden of affection, where hearts entwine,
I won't vie for your affection, your heart as a shrine.

I refuse to engage in the game of comparison,
For love is not a prize, nor a competition.
In the symphony of emotions, where souls align,
I won't fight for your attention, a love so divine.

I won't measure my worth by the depth of your gaze,
For my value lies not in the games we play.
In the quiet of self-love, where acceptance thrives,
I won't compete for your affection, where ego connives.

Love is not a battlefield, nor a conquest to claim,
It's a gentle dance, where hearts aflame.
In the sanctity of authenticity, where truth resides,
I won't compete for your love, where passion collides.

For I know my worth, beyond the need to strive,
In the depth of my soul, where love's alive.
I won't compete for you, for I cherish my peace,
In the realm of self-respect, where love finds release.